Demented

Jacky Fleming

BLOOMSBURY

First published in Great Britain 2004
This paperback edition published 2006

Copyright © 2004 by Jacky Fleming

The moral right of the author has been asserted

Bloomsbury Publishing Plc, 36 Soho Square, London W1D 3QY

A CIP catalogue record for this book is available from the British Library

ISBN 0 7475 8151 7
9780747581517

10 9 8 7 6 5 4 3 2 1

Printed in Hong Kong/China by South China Printing Co. Ltd

All papers used by Bloomsbury Publishing are natural, recyclable products made from
wood grown in well-managed forests. The manufacturing processes conform
to the environmental regulations of the country of origin.

www.bloomsbury.com/jackyfleming

please make a selection from the following options

1   friends reunited

2   middleage crisis

3   old age and death crisis

4   the credits

5   the eyetest

6   a property programme

7   because you're worth it

8   meeting Amanda

9   an estate agent

10   a consumer survey

11   a supermarket

12   mobile phone

13   tv

14   Amanda's crisis

15   more tv

16   hair crisis

17   pensions

18   the phone again

you have not made a selection   please make a selection now

 inside image: Friends Reunited

what year
did I leave....

oh my GOD I can't believe it
that's AMAZING

Amanda Schwartz!

I haven't even THOUGHT of her in 36 years

Hi Amanda,
How's the last 36 years been?

Do you still
wear plaits
and pick your nose?

Amanda runs her own
IT consultancy company...
lives in Mustique
for 6 months of the
year....

...

have I changed?

Hi Amanda,
Yes I've changed.
People say I look a
lot like Naomi Campbell
these days. Haven't
got a scanner so
can't send photo.
Your house in
Mustique looks
very nice.
Don't you miss
winter in England
though?

You have been disconnected ...OK

Not really, no.

It's more usual to disconnect at the END of something rather than the middle

but you're not from round here are you

who'd have thought it...
boring bloody Amanda pigtail Schwartz
has got a house on Mustique
and her own
consultancy...
I bet she had a
happy childhood too
...bitch

oh my god
what's happened
to my face . . . .

KENNY
quick
something
terrible's
happened

You ARE

middle-aged

Nobody warned me..

I'm not ready...

I thought it was
just another hangover..

come to think of it
I've been looking a
bit ill for...YEARS

When you rang I thought something terrible must have happened

You can't let a few wrinkles get you down – they give your face wisdom.. and character

and show you've lived a full and... somewhat decadent life

My body has begun t disintegrate. Do you real what t mean

It means I'm going to get OLDER...
and OLDER...
and then
I'm going
to die
You're not exactly
the FIRST, are you?
I mean, it's not
as though
you didn't
KNOW that,
is it?

I don't want to
die wondering what
I would have been
if I'd grown up

You'd probably be pretty much the same
only suave sophisticated competent and rich . . . .
and you might have stopped wearing
vests and kneesocks . . .
thanks

I know what's happened...
it's since you
emailed that girl
from primary school
you never liked..
admit it...
Amanda Schwartz
and her
house on
Mustique...
that's IT
isn't it
fuck off

go on then –
read them out

1st lighting technician Stubly Longfellow
2nd lighting technician Barney Greenbaum
wigs Alicia John makeup Felicity
Blythe-Dudley hair Genevieve and
Clarence best boy..

All right ALL RIGHT....

Kenny I think I may be losing my eyesight

You probably just need glasses like everyone else

But my eyesight's always been PERFECT
I don't want to be a blind cartoonist like Beethoven

which is clearer now –
the red . . . . or the green . . . . . .

the red . . . . or the green . . .

yes . . . the red.

Or the green.

You look lovely

Please don't patronise me Kenny, my days of looking lovely are over.

I may look distinguished, myopic, or tired but not lovely

my GOD the DETAIL
my eyes were NEVER this good
I wonder if I'm deaf as well —

firming anti-wrinkle cream
with added ginger...
♫ ♫ ♫ ♪ ♫ ♪ ♫ ♪

with built in non-fade
shine magnifiers...
this is big news
because you're worth it
♫ ♪♪ ♪ ♪ ♫ ♪♪ ♪ ♪♪

This week we're here
in Tuscany helping
Andrea find
her dream
holiday home

36

right place

39

because
you're worth it

because
you're
worth it

because you're worth it

because

what
are you
doing?

I can't meet her - she'll notice I'm in a state of arrested development..... what is that growing out of the bookcase?

and what would I WEAR?

the Oxfam? . . .

or Help the Aged?

isn't that what you were wearing in the first place?

and what if it is?

45

You haven't changed at ALL

damn
you
noticed

Of course I never imagined we'd become LANDLORDS, but all our friends seem to be doing it..

Anyway, enough about me
weren't you doing
something...
feminist?

oh THAT...
gosh..yes
the olden days...

49

women today ENJOY being women ...

'it's great to know what you've got and FLAUNT it ...

oh yes I love it

getting your tits out
has saved a lot
of flagging
careers

oh yes

there's always
that

young women
aren't afraid of
men ... they
can deal
with it

really?
that's fantastic...
HOW?

...and of course now that Bunty's persuaded Buzz to fly to Bergerac it's cut hours off everyone's journey. Made front page news in the Good Life. And let's face it, it wouldn't help the man in the street if Marcia and Freddy DIDN'T have a chateau near St-Céré would it? And of course the locals are delighted because they get to do some babysitting for Marcia's revolting children and we get to drink some decent wine

I'm sorry Amanda I drifted off a bit there

59

So do you feel grown up Amanda?

Grown up?
I lurch between feeling
haggard and exhausted
I've got a delinquent teenager
I dye my grey bits. I've
begun to replace my body parts
and I can't see anything smaller
than a cow...
I suppose that's
grown up

what about
the house on
Mustique?

what about
looking like
Naomi
Campbe[ll]

Last time I saw Amanda she was 11 . . .

Can you hear that burglar alarm going off again?

very much so

63

I'm sorry, I'm afraid we've got nothing with any character at the moment — they're in such demand you see. You've more of a chance if you've already sold your own home, of course and pay in cash

Of COURSE..

what a fool

I'll just go and sell it

back in a mo

¼ of a MILLION . . .

for an undesirable semi..
in an unsoughtafter location..

early viewing to
AVOID
disappointment ??

How will THAT help?

STAY AWAY
to avoid disappointment

69

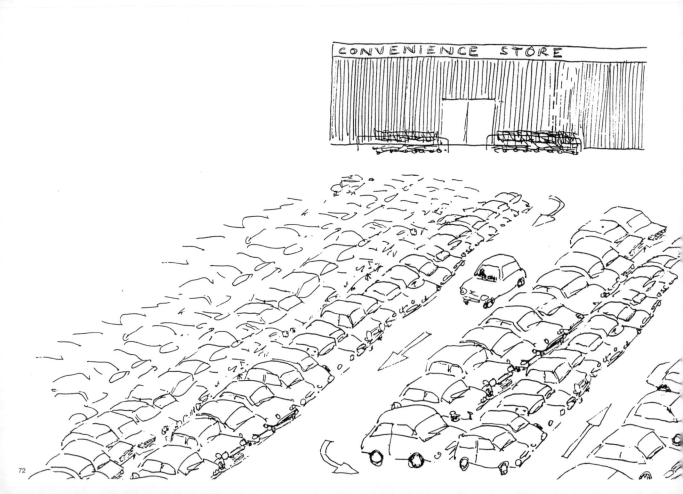

do I want the
laboratoire shampoo for
almost dead hair
or the frequent wash
shampoo for dangerously
clean hair .. ?

If I had a mobile phone
I could ring someone
and ask them ..

oh excuse me - you wouldn't have
a mobile phone I could borrow?
I just can't decide which shampoo
is the right one.. I'm sure you
know what it's like .. or not

Have you got a
loyalty card?

Have you got one of my loyalty cards, Lorraine?
I don't want to SQUANDER any unnecessary pleasantness on non-members
So how did it go with Mustique Mandy?

Her son's a dealer and she's got breast implants
Really?
Can he get us some?

the really odd thing about her was...
oops... that's my phone.. won't be a tick
aah how sweet... just got to reply..
sorry

Time you got a mobile phone ... watch this ...

oh look at that.. it tries to guess what you're going to say but gets it wrong...

that's very useful Loraine

what s t doggi later?
Fancy a ergo frigsi?

Well DO you Lorraine
fancy a ergo frigsi?

Keely says
she does
pole-dancing
to get herself
through college

Promise me, Sheila and Frank, that you're not going to revert to type the moment my back's turned and do some HIDEOUS symphony in magnolia...

I see that you have gone for the bovine magnolia look after all but with just a soupçon of imagination over the fireplace –
I have to say I don't think it works..

Amanda rang sounding a bit strange...
I'm seeing her tomorrow

What am I left with..?
a pair of
indestructible
toy breasts

and
Jonathan

I mean,

what was the point
of it all ?

That's the question

Mmm . .
what was the point when we were at school . . ?
skipping

bet you
were crap

I was not
I was very
good, as
you well
know

sorry . . . message from Roger . . .
he's in Top Shop . . . . it's all been a
terrible mistake
. . can he
come home

just got to reply . .
won't take a sec

sorry

T can sips off
t ducking
casuap?
Spell

And they're trying to teach that bloke how to chat up women. They want him to approach the girl reading by the tree oh well done, look, he's remembered everything we said... oh dear, she's run away... oh... just when he was doing so well

d'you think I should have my
face paralysed? It's OK
it was a joke

What about
a haircut?

you're not
going to do
it yourself

Are you?

You do realise that unless you come and live with me it'll never look like this again...

Well, at least you'll look nice for the rest of today

What's happened to you? Where's my frumpy friend?

I had my hair paralysed, by Laura, NVQ Level 2. but her heart wasn't in it.

I've only got the rest of today then I REVERT

I've got to say it DOES take YEARS off you...

how many?

not THAT
many...

grow up
for heaven's sake

You could almost
pass for a
grown up

There was nothing
to it really,
as there ?

Lorraine, it
didn't just revert...
it's taking revenge

I've turned into

an **AIR HOSTESS**...

Well, it's not what I call a blessing

113

115

Kenny, when my pension comes through shall we go and BLOW the lot on a pencil or an onion or something?

you haven't got a pension

sizzle

where's that teeny weeny
little h . . . .

come on out now we
haven't got all day

KNOCK
KNOCK

piss off

or I'll call
the police

where was I...

If you have a touchtone phone please press your star key twice now

WHY?

You have not pressed your star key. Please press your star key twice now

MAKE ME

If you feel your life is trickling away while your phone bill is steadily growing press **2**

If you're starting to think that running a donkey sanctuary in Provence has definite appeal press **3**

if you've completely forgotten
what you were phoning about
and which option was
which number
press **4**

if you'd like someone with an Australian accent to say
'Hello my name's Gary. How can I help you?'
in a slightly sycophantic way

press **5**

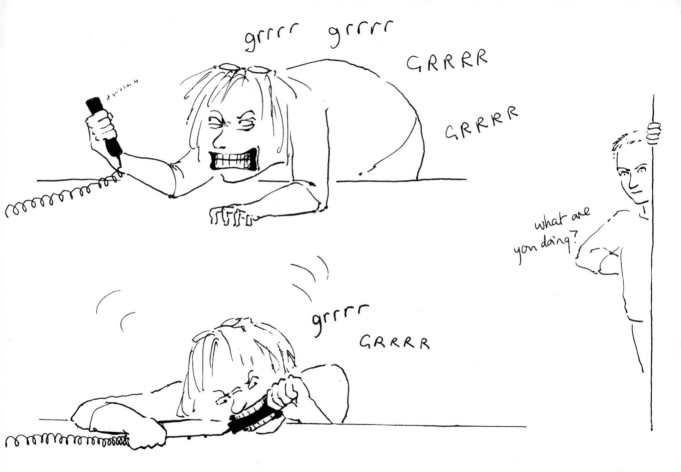

I'm hulahooping with Amanda tomorrow...
When we were 9 she could do 148..
But can she do 148 pissed and menopausal?

I DON'T think so